A Beginner's G
Mastering Computer
Networking

A Complete Overview on Windows

and Hardware Networking Made

Easy.

content within this book has been derived from various sources. Please consult a licensed professional before attempting any techniques outlined in this book.

By reading this document, the reader agrees that under no circumstances is the author responsible for any losses, direct or indirect, which are incurred as a result of the use of information contained within this document, including, but not limited to, — errors, omissions, or inaccuracies.

Table of Contents

Introduction 7

Chapter 1: Networking Basics 11

What is Computer Networking? 11

LAN vs. WAN 12

The Infrastructure of the Network 16

Client-Server vs. Peer-to-Peer 17

The Devices on the Network 20

Network Speeds 22

The Network Administrator 23

Chapter 2: The Networking Hardware You Need to Know 25

The Host Machines 25

The Network Adapter 26

The Hub 27

The Switch 28

The Router 28

The Modem 30

The Firewall 31

Chapter 3: Understanding the Network Cabling 34

Ethernet Cables 35

The Twisted Pair Cabling 36

The UTP Cables 37

The Shield Twisted Pair Cables...................................... 38

The Fiber Optic Cable 39

The Straight-Through Cables... 41

The Crossover Cables 42

Chapter 4: IP Addressing 45

The Function of Our IP Addresses.................................... 46

The Default Gateway 49

How to Find the IP Address Manually................................51

DHCP...52

The Default IP Addresses Classes 54

Chapter 5: IP Subnetting...58

Bit Borrowing 59

Determining the Host Ranges.. 61

Subnet Masks Changing.. 61

VLAN 63

Chapter 6: Common Networking Protocols...............64

The TCP/IP Model 66

Protocols of the Application Network................................ 66

Transport Layer Protocols 67

Protocols of the Internet Layer 68

Link Layer Protocols...69

The Protocol for Frame Relay....................................70

Chapter 7: Internet Essentials We Need to Know....... 72

Internet Basics 72

How to Pick Out an Internet Plan 78

Chapter 8: Virtualization and How It Fits In 83

What Does Cloud Computing Mean?..........................83

Characteristics of Cloud Computing 84

What is Virtualization?... 87

How Visualization Works in Cloud Computing 89

The Types of Cloud Services to Use.......................... 91

Should I Choose Private or Public Clouds?...............92

Chapter 9: Implementing the Windows System 95

General Features of Windows 95

What to Expect in Windows? 96

The Benefits of Using Windows 102

Implementing Windows Distributed Network 104

Conclusion 111

Introduction

Congratulations on purchasing *A Beginner's Guide to Mastering Computer Networking,* and thank you for doing so.

The following chapters will discuss all that we need to know when it is time to handle computer networking and to get it to fit our needs. Whether you are learning how to handle the computer networking for your own personal use, or you are getting the network set up to handle some of the more complex ideas that a business network will need, this guidebook is going to have the results that you are looking for. There is so much that we are able to explore when it comes to networking, and we will make sure to go through them in more detail so you can learn how to use them, and how to make it work for you.

The beginning of this guidebook is going to be all about the basics of networking. We are going to look at some of the basic elements that come with networking, such as the types of networks, the topologies, and the different components. Then we can move to the networking hardware that is necessary to put the network together, such as the switch, routers, firewalls, host machines, and more.

From there, it is time to look at how networking cabling is going to work and why this is so important. We will look at the options that come with networking cabling in particular, including the crossover cables, ethernet cables, and more. Then it is time to move our discussion over to the idea of IP addressing and what these rules and requirements are all about to keep our system safe and sound. This section will look more at the default gateway, what IP addressing is like, and how we can configure our own IP addresses as well.

In addition to IP addressing, we will spend some time looking at IP subnetting and how we are able to use this to work with some of the subnet masks, he VLAN, IPv4, and IPv6 to learn how these are going to work for some of our own codes along the way before moving into some of the common networking protocols that we need to know as well. this chapter will focus mostly on the TCP/IP protocol, along with a few of the other options that will make sure that your network is running well, and that it will be able to connect to the internet and get the connections and communications that you are looking for.

The next topic that we are going to spend some time on here is some of the essentials about the internet that we need to understand as well. This is the chapter where we learn a bit about how our networks are going to attach and communicate with the internet, how dial-up, cables, and DSL all work together, and so much more. We can then look more at virtualization and the cloud and how this cloud computing will make all of the difference when it is time to create your network and get the information and data stored in a secure manner that is easy to access.

Finally, the last thing that we are going to look at when it comes to our networks is how to implement the Windows system on our network. There are several systems that we are able to work with, but Windows is one of the best when it comes to networking, thanks to all of the features and more that are added to it for our needs. This chapter is going to look at how the Windows system works, how to implement this kind of system, and the different parts of this system that we need to focus our attention on as well.

Networking can be a complicated task. It is not uncommon for an individual, and sometimes business, to know very little when it comes to the world of networking, and they simply focus on the computer and do not question what is going on. Thanks to the information that is found in this guidebook, we are able to work around this issue and learn more about how networking can benefit us in so many ways.

Many different parts come together when we are focusing on networking and what we are able to do with this for some of our own needs as well. In addition, the goal of this guidebook was to help you to learn more about and understand how this networking can help your computer systems work together in a more efficient manner. When you are ready to learn more about computer networking for beginners, make sure to check out this guidebook to help you get started.

There are plenty of books on this subject on the market, thanks again for choosing this one! Every effort was made to ensure it is full of as much useful information as possible; please enjoy it!

Chapter 1: Networking Basics

Computer networking is considered a very wide discipline that is going to incorporate together a bunch of concepts of computing, which will be aimed at improving communication and access to some computer resources that are limited but can also be shared. This chapter is going to spend some time looking at the basics of networking and what we are able to do with this to help us get more done along the way as well.

What is Computer Networking?

The first thing that we need to look at is what computer networking is. This is a term that is able to refer back to any collection of computers that will be linked to one another to communicate and to share data, along with other information, and other resources of computing.

There are many things that we are able to do with these computing resources. In addition, some of the other resources that network also permit things like the hosts of the network to share applications, data, and many other network resources of hardware nature-file servers and printers along with many other devices that come with it.

There are a number of ways that these computer networks can be distinguished. We can look at these based on their size, functionality, and even the location. The main criterion that we need to consider here, though, is the size. The most common options that we have to notice here are the LANs and the WANs so let us look at how this is going to work.

LAN vs. WAN

LAN is going to be for our Local Area Network, and then there is the WAN, which is a bit different and is going to be the Wide Area Network. The LAN is going to be any group of computers that can be linked to one another within a smaller area, such as your building or a small office. In the LAN, there are going to be two or more computers we are able to connect together through some kind of communication media with twisted-pair copper cables, coaxial cables, and sometimes even some fiber-optic cables.

These LANs are going to be easy and less costly to work with because they are able to work with fewer computers, and you will not need to work with hardware that is as expensive as other options. The network adapters, Ethernet cables, and switches are able to be a little less expensive. The limited traffic is going to allow us to transmit data over the LAN in an easy and effective manner.

In addition, we are going to find that these LANs are going to be easier to manage since they are put into a smaller space, and even the enforcement of the security will be enhanced with the help of closer monitoring of activities that are going to happen in the same geographical location of the network. Some of the examples of these will include the home-based networks and office networks that you may use.

LANs are going to have some obvious advantages over the WANs since they are able to cover a smaller area, while the WAN is going to stretch over a larger geographical area. There are a number of benefits of working with the LAN, and these will include:

1. This is an easy network to set up because it is going to just involve a small area within which you can connect the computers that you would like. The limited area of operation is going to result in us having a limited number of machines that are networked, which is going to make it easier to set this all u.
2. This network is easy to maintain due to the small network area and a few networked computers.
3. This is an easier network to keep secure because it is working in a smaller operating environment, and there will not be as many networked devices to work with.

There are a few limitations of working with this kind of network. The main issue is that it is confined to a limited geographical space and the number of networked machines. This is going to mean that the limitation of the LAN is going to be that it is unable to accommodate that many users, so it has to be restructured to places like the home, learning spaces, some smaller settings, and small offices as well.

Then we can move on to the WAN. This is going to be a network that will stretch over a larger geographical region. It could include states, cities, and sometimes even countries. It is going to be bigger than the LAN and will not have the same restrictions when it comes to geography. It could span over a really large area with the use of satellite links, fiber optic cables, and telephone lines. The Internet is going to be a good example of how the WAN is able to work across the world.

There are many options when we work with the WAN because of how far they are able to reach. These are going to be embraced in many situations, including large business activities, government, and education. The Internet is one of the most common examples of the WAN.

There are a few different advantages that come with the WAN and choosing to work with this compared to some of the other options out there. Some of the benefits of the WAN will include:

1. These are going to be able to cover up large geographical locations and can reach out to a lot of the human population. Think about how much the Internet is able to

affect the lives of other people, and you will see how these are able to benefit us as well.

2. It can also centralize the data that we are working with. WANs are going to help support data centralization. This eliminates the need for an individual to go out and purchase back-up servers for their files and emails.

3. Getting files that are updated. Programmers are able to get the files they need to be updated within seconds because the software is able to work on a live server.

4. The quick exchange of messages. WANs are going to rely on sophisticated tools and technologies that will enable the exchange of messages t to happen faster than with other kinds of networks. Communicating on Facebook and Skype are good examples of this.

5. WANs are going to allow us to share our resources and our software. It is possible now to work on sharing RAM, hard drives, and other resources thanks to these networks.

6. Businesses are no longer going to need to worry about borders. Even when these companies are separated by large distances, they will be able to work with the Internet and communicate with one another.

7. High bandwidth. The use of leased lines that a company can use will ensure that their bandwidth is higher. This is going to increase the rates of data transfer, which will increase how productive the company can be.

A few disadvantages are going to come with this one. For example, because the networks are so big, we will find that the security issues are going to increase as well. The costs of installing this are going to be higher as well because you need many different software applications to get things done. In addition, when it comes to network troubleshooting, it is going to be a big concern because the network is going to be over a large location.

The Infrastructure of the Network

The next thing that we need to look at is the network infrastructure. This is going to hold onto all of the resources that are necessary to lead to the networking concept working to its full functionality. This means that it is going to include the design functions, human input, network protocols, software, and hardware that are needed in order to lead an effective network communication, management, and operation.

The hardware aspect of this network is important because it allows our users to physically link to all of the devices in the network while using the interface to gain access to the resources of the network. For the most part, this hardware is going to be all of the physical components that go with the network. This could include the computers or the host machine, the connecting devices that are the switches, hubs, routers, and some of the other peripherals that go with it, including the file servers, network cameras, wireless modems, and printers.

Then we are able to move on to the software of our network, and it will usually include the Network Operating System that helps run the whole thing. However, it is sometimes not necessary depending on the network nature. If you are working with something, like peer to peer network arrangement. Besides, the NOS, there are going to be numerous software applications that are going to be installed so that they can operate on host machines that networks are going to use in order to handle the tasks of that network.

The next thing that we need to work with here is the network protocols. This is going to refer to the standards and policies that are going to offer details on how network communication is able to take place. To keep it simple, the protocol is just going to be a set of conventions, procedures, rules, and other regulations that are going to govern the process of network communication. It is possible to work with these network protocols to keep the security and the safety of that network up and running.

Client-Server vs. Peer-to-Peer

The next thing that we need to consider is the difference between the peer to peer and the client to server networks. First is the peer-to-peer network architecture. In this kind of system, all of the computers are going to be connected with one another. All of the computers on this network are going to have the same amount and types of privileges, and they will share the responsibility of data processing on terms that are equal.

This is a form of computer networking that is the best for some of the smaller networks, and it usually does not support more than ten computers. The architecture is not going to provide for any kind of server role. In addition, there will be some special permissions are granted through an assignment to each computer. There are some issues with this one, though when the resources do break down or start to malfunction.

We will see a few benefits with this kind of option, though. To start, some of the benefits will include:

1. It is not as expensive to work with because there is not a dedicated server that has to go along with it.
2. The network is going to be small, which means that getting it set up and managing it is going to be pretty easy.
3. When one machine does fail, it is not going to end up affecting how well the others are able to function. This makes it more reliable.

However, a few negatives are going to show up when we work with this one. First, they are not going to have any kind of centralized system. This means that there is not going to be a mechanism in place to backup your data when it is in many different locations. In addition, there will not be any managed security because the individual computer has to go through and handle the security on its own.

Then there is the client-server option. This is going to be a network that will rely on the server, or a central computer, for allocating the resources and enforcing the security of the system. The server is able to handle all of the general network management, resource management, and security management. Then we have the other side of it where the client computers are able to communicate with one another through that central server or computer.

For example, if the client "A" wants to send over data to client "B," then that client needs to submit in a request to get permission out of the server. Then the server is able to answer back by granting permission or taking that permission away. When the server grants permission, then the communication is able to start. The benefits that we are able to work with when we focus on the client-server network includes:

1. It is easy to work with the backup of the data since we are working with a centralized system.
2. A dedicated server is able to improve the overall performance through the proper management and organization of the network resources.
3. The enforcement that you will see with the security is a lot higher because the central computer we are working with is going to be able to administer all of the resources that are shared here.
4. The speed that we are able to see with the resource sharing is going to be higher thanks to the orderly handling of all the requests that come in.

Of course, we also need to look at some of the negatives that come with this kind of network. The dedicated servers that you may work with here are going to be expensive, which can make it more costly compared to some of the other options. In addition, being able to administer to this network is something that only skilled personnel is able to do.

The Devices on the Network

From a physical perspective, it is possible that a network could be something that is simple, including just two computers that are connected with one another using an ethernet cable. However, the network is not going to stay simple all of the time. This is why we should consider any network that we work with as the building block at the start, and then see that it is going to grow over time.

Even if the network that you plan to use is going to just be one for a small office or for a home office, you may need to take into account what you would like to do with this network at some point in the future. You could then go through and figure out how you would be able to accommodate these needs later on. Doing this is going to make the network last for you a bit longer and will eliminate some future frustrations that can come up when you hook up a new server without having to change it all up. Some of the different parts that we need to consider and that may be necessary parts to add to our network later includes:

1. The client workstations and PCs
2. Database hosts
3. Printers.
4. File servers
5. Any of the additional devices that you will want to add to the system later on as well, including the notebooks, handhelds, and laptops.
6. Other peripheral hardware including the removable media, network and the end-user software, web cameras, networking switching and routing components, hard drives, and interface drives.

Network Speeds

When we look at computer networking, you will find that the bandwidth and the speed are going to be used in an interchangeable manner, but they are different ideas. The speed of the network is going to be the circuitry bit rate, and then the bandwidth is the speed that you end up being able to use. The speed is going to be more of the theoretical throughput, while bandwidth is going to be the actual throughput.

When we are working with the internet, there are ways that we are able to define the speed (or the bandwidth in actuality), including some of the following:

1. How slow or fast the new connection that you are working with that is established.
2. How long it is going to take to stream video content in a comfortable manner.
3. How fast it is going to take to download any of the content that comes from the websites you use.
4. How fast or slow it takes us to get that web page to open up.

You will quickly find that the bandwidth is going to play a big role when it comes to figuring out the speed that comes with the network. In computer networking, it is common to say that the bandwidth is going to be the rate of the data that happens with the connection. These bandwidths are going to vary quite a bit, going from a few megabytes a second to thousands of them. Different standards of Wi-Fi are going to help us to figure out what the different bandwidths will be, along with some of the other technologies of networking.

The Network Administrator

For a network in order to serve the function that we want, there is going to be someone who is going to be responsible for working on the network and making sure that it behaves in the manner that we would like. This person is often going to go behind the scenes of the network and will be known as the administrator of that network. This network administrator is often going to be behind the scenes and will make sure that there are not any bugs in the system, that it is working properly, and that the network is up to date all of the time.

There are many tasks that the network administrator is going to focus on in order to get their job done. This could take some time to go through all of the options, but some of the main tasks that this administrator is going to work with will include:

1. The management of the network storage in a physical sense while also helping with keeping the cloud up and running.
2. Basic testing and security measures to make sure that the program stays safe.
3. Offering the necessary assistance to the architects of the network with network models that will design the work.
4. The server management and various operating systems to get work done.
5. The process of updating and deploying any of the software that is needed.
6. Troubleshooting and fixing issues with the network when they do show up.
7. Doing any of the repair work that shows up and doing the necessary upgrades of the network.
8. A configuration of the software in the network, including the servers, routers, and switches.

In order to handle all of these tasks and more, the network administrator has to be highly knowledgeable in these networks and have skills in the world of IT. It is preferable if they are able to do well with computer networking. They also need to be able to think in a critical manner and possess some strong analytical skills so that they can do some of the network issues of the computer in an effective manner.

Chapter 2: The Networking Hardware You Need to Know

Though the physical and software components of the network are going to be important as well, our focus here is going to be more about the physical components, so we learn more about what they are and how they work. To start with, the physical computer is going to host the machines, which will be the computers, routers, hubs, switches, repeaters, Network Interface Cards, modems, network servers, and any other devices that we try to add to the network.

The Host Machines

These are going to include the workstations that we use and any computers that are found on the network. The host machines or computers can include our laptops and desktop computers along with some portable devices (including our tablets and phones), and any of the additional accessories that come with these. This means if you hook up a mouse, keyboard, CD player, hard drive that is portable or something else into the system, then it is going to count as part of the hardware.

Computers, of course, are going to be the primary part of our network because the network will not survive without it. Computers work well because they provide us with a platform to use to perform all of the tasks that we want to handle on this network. In case there is a centralized system present, the computers are there to serve as a link between the users and the dedicated network server as well.

The Network Adapter

These are sometimes known as the network interface card that we talked about before. This network adapter, or NIC, is going to be a component of the hardware that will link one computer over to another within the same network as well. This NIC is going to support the transfer rates of the network from about 10 Mbps to 1000Mbps.

All of the cards that are used on the network will be assigned their own unique addresses by the IEEE. These addresses are going to be seen as the physical or the MAC addresses, and are used to help us identify which computers are on that network as well. You will find that there are going to be two forms of these network cards that we are able to focus on including:

1. The Wireless Network Adapter: This is going to come with an antenna that you are able to work in order to grab a connection over to the wireless network. For the laptop that you are using, it is common that there will be a NIC that is built into it, but there are some desktops that will require us to go through and install this on our own.

2. Wired Network Adapter: This is going to be something that is fixed into the motherboard of almost all computers that you want to work with. Cables, as well as connectors, are going to be used to transfer all of the data when we work with one of these types of network cards.

The Hub

The next thing on our list is going to be the Hub. This is there to help divide the connection of the network into several devices. A hub is going to connect all of the computers that are on the same network through some cables. Each computer is going to send out a request to the network and will use the hub to make this possible.

Any time that the hub is able to receive a new request from a computer; it is going to broadcast out that request across the network to all of the other devices that are connected. Each of the devices will do a check to see if that message belongs there. If not, then the request is going to be discarded and not used at all.

The biggest downside that we are going to see with this process is that it is going to use up a lot more bandwidth, and the communication that we work with is going to be limited in the process. Right now, the hub is not used as much because most computers have made a move over to the routers and switches, which we will talk about next.

The Switch

This is going to help us link a number of devices on the network with one another. This important connection is going to be more advanced than what we see with the hub and will get a similar job done in a more efficient and fast manner. The switch, for example, has an update that is going to help determine what the destination of the transmitted data should go. The switch is then able to transmit the message to the right destination based on the physical address to the incoming request.

Unlike what we saw with the hub, this switch is not going to transmit data to every computer or device that is on the network. This means that there is going to be faster speeds of the data since the individual computers because the individual computers are going to be able to communicate right with the switch instead.

The Router

A router is going to provide us with the internet connection that we need to the local area network we are using. It is going to receive, analyze, and forward all of the incoming packets to another computer network as well. When we look at the OSI model, it is going to be known as Layer 3 or the network layer.

Packet forwarding is going to be governed hereby the contents that we find in the routing table. The router is going to be smart enough in all of this to choose or decide the best path for the transmission of the data through all of the paths that are there.

There will be a number of benefits to the router, and these are going to include some of the following:

1. This method is going to provide us with a higher level of security when it comes to transmitting the information and the data. The message is only going to head over to the device where it belongs, not to everyone.
2. It is going to be a reliable option to use because the breaking down or the malfunctioning of this router is only going to slow the network down, but any of the networks that are not served by this router will not be affected at all.
3. A router is going to help improve the performance of the router overall. This will ensure that the network performs in the manner that we want and that there are no problems along the way.
4. The routers are going allow us to have a larger range in our network, with little concern over performance issues.

There are a few limitations to using the routers, so they are not something that is going to work all of the time. For example, they are more expensive to work with, and if the costs of your network are already high, then this is not something that most people are willing to work with. There is also the need to have skilled personnel working with these as well because they are a bit harder to handle compared to other options.

The Modem

Next on our list here is going to be the modem. This is actually going to be more of an acronym for Modulator/Demodulator. It is going to change some of the digital data that you have into analog signals through a telephone line. The modem is going to make it possible to establish the connection that we want to the Internet, working with the telephone line that is there. It is then installed into the PCI slow of the motherboard, not on the motherboard on its own.

There are a few ways that we are able to classify our modems. Ad usually, they will be classified based on the rates that they can transmit the data and the speeds that are present with this. Some of the ways that we are able to classify our modems will include:

1. The cable modem
2. The cellular modem
3. The dial-up modem or the standard PC modem.

30

The Firewall

We also need to understand how the firewall is going to fit into all of this. We are able to work with a firewall that is in the form of hardware, but it also turns up as software in some cases as well. Either way, the firewall is going to be an application or a network device that is going to restrict the entry of who goes into and out of a network that is private. These private networks will usually need to be connected to the internet.

These firewalls can be useful when there is some need present to restrict the users of the network from gaining unauthorized entry into the network, or just to make sure that the hacker is not able to get on or start a denial of service attack. When the messages are being transmitted in and out of the internet, they are going to pass through the firewall to be screened. Those that do not meet the requirements of the firewall are not going to be allowed through.

It should be noted here that the firewalls are not there to offer us any kind of authentication services outside of traffic screening and network connection permissions. This means that they need to be complemented in order to guarantee that there is an enhanced amount of security on our network at all times.

As we go through this, you will notice that there are a number of firewalls that we are able to work with. These will include the following:

1. Packet-filtering firewalls. These ones are going to examine the packets that either leave or enter the network and then will only allow those that meet the permitted threshold to come in.

2. Circuit-level gateway: This security measure is applicable to the establishment of the TCP or UDP connection. The packets that flow unchecked once the connection has been established.

3. Proxy server firewalls: This proxy server is important because it will establish the connectivity to the internet and then will submit requests on behalf of the host machine. There is a way in which these proxies are going to be configured in order to filter the traffic that will go through them.

4. Web application firewalls: These are going to be the ones that are able to set the rules to the HTTP conversations. The rules are going to be customized in order to identify some of the potential attacks that could come in, with the goal of blocking them if possible.

All of these different parts of hardware are going to be important to what we are trying to do when it comes to working with the networking process. The hardware ensures that we are actually able to work with the network that we are on, and will give us some of the physical features that we are used to interacting with when we do our network.

Chapter 3: Understanding the Network Cabling

The next thing that we are going to look at is known as network cabling. This is one of the most important aspects when it comes to a computer network. Cables are going to provide us with the physical connections that we need between the different components that help with interconnection and to serve as the communication media that we are looking for. IN other words, cabling is going to be used in order to establish some of the links that we need outside of offering a medium through which packets are transmitted from source to a designated destination.

Cables are going to be something that is classified based on the type and the function. In particular, we are going to use these Ethernet cables for most of the networking tasks that we would like to accomplish. That is why we are going to spend some time discussing the different network cables that we are able to focus on.

Ethernet Cables

Ethernet cabling is going to come with three common types of cables that we are able to work with. These include the fiber optic cables, the twisted pair copper, and the coaxial. The first option that we are going to look at is coaxial. In many cases, access to the internet is going to be achieved with this kind of cabling. The term is going to be analogous to the fact that there are going to be two conductors that we work with that will run parallel to one another along the way.

These cables are going to contain some conductors that are able to run through the center of the cables. There will also be a layer of insulation that will be able to help us out by surrounding the conductor. In addition, there is going to be a conducting shield that is right after our insulating material. This material, along with the conducting shield, will make these highly resistant when it comes to interference from the external environment along the way.

These cables are going to be categorized more on the thinnet and the thicknet types. The thinnet is simply going to be the thin ethernet option, and then the thicknet will be the thick ethernet option that we are able to work with. Of course, we have to remember that both of these are going to be kind of outdated forms of cabling techniques that we will find with the Ethernet that we are going to work with.

Another thing that we need to consider when doing some of the work that we want with these coaxial cables is some of the main characteristics that come with them. Some of the main characteristics that are found with these coaxial cables include:

1. This kind of cable is going to consist of two materials that are conducting and are able to run parallel to one another
2. The two conductors are going to include both the inner and the outer conductors. The inner conductor is going to be important because it is going to have a single copper wire to move the message, and then the outer conductor is going to have a copper mesh. The two are going to be separated out with a non-conductor in the process
3. The middle core is going to be responsible for the transmission of the data where the outer copper mesh is going to protect things against any EMI or electromagnetic interference.
4. Compared to some of the twisted pair cables, you will find that these are going to be cables that come in with a higher frequency.

The Twisted Pair Cabling

Another option that we are able to look at is going to be known as a twisted pair cable. These are going to come with four different types of copper wires that work together. All four of these wires are going to twist around one another. The twisting is going to aim at reducing some of the external interference and crosstalk. This cable type is going to be used in many of the implementations of LAN.

The twisted-pair cables are often used with both the network cabling and the telephone cabling. These are going to be then classified into either the Shielded Pair Cables or the Unshielded Twisted Pair cables.

The UTP Cables

We can also work with what is known as the UTP cables. These are going to be embraced for use in things like telecommunication. They are going to fall into a few different categories based on what we would like to accomplish in the process. Some of the categories are going to include:

1. Category 1: This is going to be used quite a bit and is a low-speed data telephone line.
2. Category 2: This one is able to support speeds of our data that go up to 4 Mbps.
3. Category 3: This one can go a bit faster. It is able to support the speed of data that goes up to 16 Mbps.

4. Category 4: This one is able to help us with speeds of our data up to 20 Mbps, and we will often see that it is used for data transmissions that need to be done over a long distance.
5. Category 5: This one is going to be able to support up to 200 Mbps and can even allow us to go through longer distances compared to what we see with the other options.

There are several benefits that we are going to see when it comes to these kinds of cables. First, they are going to be pretty cheap to work with. They are also efficient enough that we can work with them on the LANs that we want to focus on, and it is easy to install some of these cables along the way.

Finally, there are some limitations that we are going to find when we want to work with these kinds of cables as well. The main issue that we are going to find is that they will be a bit limited when they are sent over shorter distances. This is often because they are more prone to attenuation as well.

The Shield Twisted Pair Cables

Another option that we are able to focus on here is the shielded twisted pair cables. These ones are going to have an insulating kind of mesh that is able to surround the conducting copper wire for an enhanced experience when it comes to data transmissions. They are going to be characterized by some of the following:

1. They are vulnerable to attenuation. This means that there is a need for shielding along the way.
2. Shielding is going to help us to make sure that we get a higher rate of transmission along the way.
3. These are easy cables that we are able to install along the way.
4. These are moderate when it comes to the costs that we see, so it will not be so bad to work with compared to some of the other options.
5. These are able to accommodate some of the higher data capacities that we would like to work with for transmission than the unshielded twisted pair cables.

There are going to be a few limitations that we are going to see when we work with these kinds of cables. They are going to be a bit more expensive than what we will see with some of the unshielded twisted pair cables. In addition, they are going to be highly prone to attenuation as well.

The Fiber Optic Cable

The next type of cable that we are going to look at is known as the fiber optic cable. This is going to be the type of cable that is going to work with electrical signals for some of the data transmissions that we want to work with. The cable is able to hold onto some optical fibers with a coating in plastic so that the data can be sent out with pulses of light. The plastic coating is going to be highly helpful because it is going to make sure that these cables are protected against interference from electromagnets and from high heats. The transmissions that come with these fiber optic cables are going to be faster compared to some of the other options.

A few elements are going to show up when we work with this kind of cable along the way. There are three main parts that we are going to concentrate on, including the core, jacket, and cladding.

The first part here is the core. This is simply going to be a narrow strand made up of glass or plastic for the transmission of light. The amount of light that is able to pass through this fiber is going to increase based on the size of our core.

Then there is the cladding. This is going to be the concentric layer that we find with the glass. It is going to offer us a lower refractive index at the interface of the core in order to make sure that the light waves are able to go through the fiber the way that we need.

Finally, the third part is going to be the jacket. This is simply a plastic coating for protection so that the strength of the fiber is preserved. It also will absorb some of the shock and offers protection for the fiber.

We can also look at some of the advantages that come with this kind of cable including:

1. The greater bandwidth: These kinds of cables are going to offer us a lot more bandwidth. This means that they are able to transmit some more data compared to some of the copper cables that we talked about before.
2. Faster speeds: These cables are able to transmit all of our data in the form of signals of light. This is going to make some of the optic data transmissions really fast and high compared to what we see with other options like twisted-pair copper cables.
3. Data transmissions are going to occur over some longer distances compared to the twisted pair of copper cables.
4. These fiber optic cables are less prone to attenuation. This means that the fiber optic cables are going to be more reliable compared to the twisted pair cables.
5. These cables are going to be stronger and thinner compared to the others. This helps them to handle more pull pressure and other things compared to other cable options.

The Straight-Through Cables

Another thing that we need to consider is the straight-through cables. This is going to be an example of one of the twisted-pair copper cables that are going to connect our computer, or another network host, over to the router, switch, and the hub that we are using. We are also able to refer to this kind of cable to a patch cable as well.

A patch cable is going to be another option for a wireless connection in a case where a single, and sometimes more, host machines are going to try to connect over to the router through the wireless signal. Pins are going to match on the patch cable. This is going to use a single wire to do this that is standard and will follow the necessary wiring standards for T568A or T568B.

The Crossover Cables

We can also look at the crossover cables. This is going to be a type of cable that will form up any Ethernet cable that will provide us with a direct link between the different devices that are on our network. This is often going to be referred to as the RJ45 cable. It is going to work with a few different wiring standards when it comes to the terminal points. For example, it is going to use the T568A on one end and then the T568B on the other end.

The internal wiring that we will see with this one is going to receives and transmits the signals. It is also going to connect together some of the networking devices that are similar. We will find, in some examples, that we can work with the crossover cable so that we are able to connect together one computer to another computer, or one switch over to another switch.

We are able to compare the two of these together pretty well as well. To keep it simple, the straight-through cables are there to help us to link dissimilar networking devices with one another, and then we would use the crossover cables to help us to link together devices that are similar to one another. Some of the reasons that you would want to work with the straight-through cables would include:

1. The switch to router
2. Hub to server
3. Switch to computer
4. Hub to computer
5. Switch to server

Then there are times when we will want to work with the crossover cables as well. These are going to be important when we work with the following kinds of device connection scenarios.

1. PC NIC to router ethernet port NIC
2. Router to router
3. Switch over to another switch
4. Switch to hub
5. PC to PC
6. Hub to hub

Then the last topic that we need to spend some time to look through in this chapter is the rollover cables. This is going to be known as the rollover wired cables. They are going to end up with some opposite pin alignments on the terminal ends. This means that it is the first pin that is on the connector A is able to link with the pin 8 in the connector B.

These rollover wired cables are going to sometimes be known as the YOST cables and are used to help link some of the networking devices console port so that it is something that we can reprogram. While the straight-through cables and the crossover cables are intended to handle the transmission of our data, the rollover cable is going to be used to help us create a new interface with a given networking device.

Knowing how to work with the different cables that are present will be important when it comes to helping us get some good results in the process with our network. These cables are going to take some of our time and attention so that we know which ones are necessary for the cables that we want to do, and for ensuring that we are using the right kinds based on the network that we use and what kind of data we want to send over as well.

Chapter 4: IP Addressing

The next topic that we are going to look at is some of the basics that come with these IP addresses. An IP address is going to be a digital address that comes in at 32 bits that, when we write it out, is going to look like something similar to 10.156.158.12. An IP is going to be a set of numbers that will be used to help us to identify a computer, or another network device, with the help of the IP, or the Internet Protocol for the communication of that network. The value for any of the sets that are found in this address will fall somewhere between 0 and 255.

This address is going to be somewhat similar to what we see with a phone number. Let us say that you would like to call up your friend. You would just use their phone number to call them up and make sure that the phone sent you right to them. The computers and the switching equipment for your phone company would be able to look at the number and will ensure that the ringing and the transmission are sent to the right place.

Once the connection has happened, as long as you worked with the right phone number, you will be able to talk to the person that you want. When you do talk to these people through your hone, the audio is going to carry a signal, and the phone is going to travel over a pair of copper wires from the location where you do the phone call all the way over to the switch that your phone company nearby has. From this location, the signal can be converted to a light wave in order to travel on over to a fiber optic cable to reach another switch as well. This process will continue until it gets near the location where you want to send that data.

Therefore, when the signal gets near the location where you are trying to send it, the process will convert that back to an audio analog signal, with the help of traveling over a pair of copper wires from the phone company in that location to the house of the person you want to call. The landline will work this way. There are some differences that we are going to see when it comes to doing this same process with a cell phone, but the idea is going to be similar

The Function of Our IP Addresses

In a manner that is really similar to what we saw with the example above and phone numbers, the IP address is going to help with some of the connections that happen between the computer hosts and the routing equipment that is there as well. To put this in another way, if two computers online have the IP address of one another, it is easy for them to communicate with one another. Unlike what we see with the phones though, which will use switching equipment to help with the connections, computers are able to connect to one another over the Internet with the help of routing equipment, which is going to share the paths of communication with thousands or hundreds of other computers as well.

When we are able to relay the data from our computer to the router, then it is going to be the job of the router to find where a short and open path for communication with another router is going to be present. We want to make sure to pick out one that is not only close but will also connect us to the computer that we are using as the destination. The router will be able to do this with the help of the routes that are the defaults, or when it decides to learn dynamically and uses recording tables, called routing tables, to help it keep track of which of these IP addresses are present on any of the routers communication pots along the way.

Because all of our routers are going to be connected to each other on the Internet, and this connection is often going to look similar to what we see with the web of a spider, data is able to travel over a lot of paths or routes to help it get to the right destination. If one of the routers or some of the links that are connecting are going to be offline, then other routers will try to move this data in order to find a brand new route for this kind of destination. To make sure that this method of dynamic communication happens, these routers are handed an IP address as well to make finding one another a little bit easier.

Understanding the Binary Number System

Before we go into too many details of how binary is going to work, we first need to define what the binary system is all about when it comes to computing in the first place. Therefore, this brings us to the point of what is the binary number system. This is going to be known as a base-2 number system. One Gottfried Leibnix originally invented this system. This system, analogous to the name, is going to be composed of just two numbers, 0 and 1, and will form the basis for what we see with all of the binary codes that we want to write. To keep things simple, binary code is going to be the only code that machines are able to read in these systems.

We can see this binary in action pretty well. The electrical ON and OFF signals are going to be represented by 1 and 0, respectively. When one adds 1 to 1, they are going to move one spat over to the left into the 2's place. They will then put the 0 into the 1's place. The outcome here is going to be 10. So, something that is different from the decimal number system where we find that 10 is equal to ten, a 10 is going to represent 20 in this kind of system.

If we consider how popular this decimal number system is, we can then place values that begin with 1s and then move steadily over to 10s, 100s, and 1000s as we go to the left. This is often as a result of our decimal system is based on the power of 10. In a similar manner, the place values in this system are going, to begin with,

1s to 2s, 4s, 8s, and 16s going left and in that order. This is simply because the binary system is going to operate with the powers of 2. The binary digits, which are 0 and 1, are going to be known as bits.

The Default Gateway

The next thing that we need to work with is the default gateway. This is going to be the nodes of the network that are used by the IP suite to act as a router and will forward on packets to the computer in different networks unless there will be path specifications that are able to match with the IP address of the network host that is receiving the message in the first place.

It is important for us to be able to figure out how to find the IP address of the network's default so that we are able to troubleshoot the program pretty well and to make sure that we are able to gain access to some of the web-based management of the router. In most cases, the router's private IP address is going to be the same as the default gateway's IP address. It is going to be the IP address with which a router is able to communicate with another local network. However, we can find that the private IP address that shows up is not always the default gateway here. This means that we may need to go through and find it in some manner.

The good news here is that there are some steps that we are able to work in order to make sure that we will find the IP address that we need for the default gateway. The steps that we are going to look out for this below are going to help us to find this default gateway for the MS Windows version, but the other options are going to be similar along the way as well. The steps that we can utilize for this one include:

1. Open up your Control Panel.
2. When you are in there, you can select Network and Internet.
3. From there, we are able to click on the Network and Sharing Center.
4. Select the setting to Change Adapter
5. Traceback your default gateway's IP connection here.
6. Now we want to double click on these network connections. This is going to open up the Wi-Fi status, the Ethernet status, or another dialog based on the kind of network that we want to work with.
7. When you have clicked on that, select the Details.
8. Locate the IPv4 Default gateway. Depending on the IP address or IP that you are using, you may need to look for the IPv6 Default Gateway instead.
9. This IP address should show up in the value column. Note this address.
10. You should now be able to use this IP address to help you out when it is time to do a troubleshoot of the issues to

connection on your network, to access the router if you want, or to handle the other functions that you want to do.

How to Find the IP Address Manually

Now, there are times when you will need to go through and know ahead of time what the IP address is for your machine. There is a way that you are able to manually find this address if it is needed. A simple way that we are able to find what IP address is assigned to your machine. The steps that we are able to use for this one include:

1. Open up the CMD prompt. We are able to do this by clicking on the Start button and then Run. Then we are able to type in "cmd" and press on the ENTER key.
2. Now we are able to type in command of ipconfig/all into the command that we opened up before.

When this is done, we should be able to see a window that is going to show us the IP addresses that are on our computer along with the addresses on our DNS servers, default gateway, and the subnet mask. There should be other information that is important to the network as well.

In addition, there are a few other things that you are able to do with this process as well. To start, we can work with Pinging the IP address of our router. This is with the assumption that you know what it is in the first place. To ping this address for the router, you will open up the command prompt, using the steps that we talked about in the first option. Then the information that shows up in the CMD prompt should be able to tell us whether or not the machine is already configured to handle that IP address or not.

DHCP

Another option that we are going to work with is DHCP. This is going to be short for the Dynamic Host Configuration Protocol. This protocol will provide us with swift, automatic, and centralized IP address allocation within our network. It is also going to be used in order to help with the proper configuration of the default gateway, the subnet mask, and the DNS server, to name a few.

This server is important because it is going to issue us a unique IP address and will construct some of the other network information in a more automatic manner for us. While a lot of homes and small businesses are going to rely on these routers in order to get them to perform the functions of this kind of server, the implementations that we see with the large networks could make sure of the single dedicated computer to get the same kind of work done.

Clients who are on the routed networks request for IP addresses from the routers. These routers are then going to respond when they assign the available IP addresses to the network devices that originally sent the request. The requesting devices have to be turned on and then connected back to the network. In addition, the request has to be directed back to the server. This request is going to be known more as a DHCPDISCOVER request.

This request is going to be found inside of the packet known as DISCOVER. The server is then able to respond when it provides the client with an IP address with this packet. The network device is then going to respond when it accepts that offer. If the server is able to find it suitable to confirm this address assignment over to the said device, it is going to then send out an ACK to the device that was given that address. However, if it finds that this is not a suitable kind of transmission, then it is going to send it back.

There are a few benefits that we are going to see this kind of server process. First, the use of this is going to eliminate any of the chances of the risks of assigning the same IP to more than one of the devices on the same network. In addition, the dynamic IP address allocation is going to make managing this network quite easy for the administrators, which is always positive.

A few issues can show up with this one though as well. To start, all of the devices or the computers that are on the network have to be configured in the proper manner so that they are able to get an IP address form this server. In addition, they have to get that IP address in order to communicate back with the network. In addition, the always changing IP addresses for these stationary devices, including printers, is something that is not very necessary and can be seen as a waste.

The Default IP Addresses Classes

There are going to be quite a few of these classes for IP addresses that are in the IP hierarchy. The IPv4 addressing system is able to come through and will find five different classes that show up, including Class A, Class B, Class C, Class D, and Class E. Let us look at what we are going to see with each of these.

The first option is going to be Class A. This is going to be a class of IP addresses that we are able to identify with some of the features that are below:

1. The first bit that comes with the first octet in this network is always going to be found as 0. This means that the first octet of the network address is going to be found within the range of 1 and 127.
2. The class A address is only gonged to include the IP addresses that begin with 1.X.X.X up to 126.X.X.X.
3. Some of the loopback IP addresses are going to be taken care of when we are working with the IP range of 127.x.x.x.
4. The default subnet mask that we see with this address is going to be 255.0.0.0. This means that class A address network can only handle up to 126 networks.

From there, we are going to work with the class B address. This one is a bit different, and some of the key features that we are able to handle this kind of IP address will include:

1. The class B addresses are going to have two bits of the first octet, and these are set at one and zero. They can range between 128.x.x.x to 191.255.x.x.
2. The network addresses that are found in this class are going to be 2 to the 14th power.
3. There is a possibility of 65534 host addresses on each network when we work with this one.

Then we are able to move on to the C address option as well. This one is going to be able to take on a bit more work compared to the others. For example, the first three bits that we are going to see in the first octet in this one will be set up to 110 based on what you are using, and the range is going to be higher.

With Class D, the addresses are going to include the first octet being 1110 as the first four bits that you are working with. This is going to specifically be a class that is there to help outwit multicasting. This process of multicasting is going to involve the transmission of data, not to one host or to two, but to many hosts. This is going to be the reason why it is not necessary for us to go through and extract the host addresses from the IP addresses for class D. There is also not going to be the possibility for the subnet mask for Class D.

Then, we can end out with the Class E. This IP address is going to be set aside for some special functions. For example, it is often used to help with experimental functions, study, or R&D. The IP addresses that show up in this option are going to be a bit higher compared to some of the others, but it is going to be similar to the Class D option, this one is not going to come with a subnet mask.

These IP addresses are going to be important to some of the work that we want to be done along the way. We will find that they will make it easier for computers on the same network, and even computers that are not on the same network, to communicate with one another along the way. Being able to go through and understanding these IP addresses and even where they are located and where you can find them on your own computer is going to be important to ensure that you get the best results along the way.

Chapter 5: IP Subnetting

Another topic that we need to look at here is going to be known as subnetting. Routed IP environments that we want to work with are going to require that we are able to pool together the IP addresses, and then these need to be subnetted to make sure that they will work. This is important because it allows each sub-net to see itself as a discrete segment of the larger internetwork that they are in. the router is tenable to tie together all of the different sub-nets into one network. The router already knows how to route the traffic in the correct way to go to the right segments because it is going to be able to build up a routing table. This table is going to be what is responsible for networking the road map that we use.

While this is an important process to work with, we have to remember that IP sub-netting is going to be pretty complex and to make this as informative as possible, but still, something that we are able to understand, we are going to just focus on the subnetting that happens in one IP address class overall. We are going to look at how we are able to work with doing this with Class B IP addresses because it is a bit easier compared to some of the others.

The first thing to consider here is that the sub-netting is going to be a two-part process. First, we need to determine what the subnet mask is for our network. Remember that this is going to turn out to be something different than we see with the default subnet masks. After we figure out what this mask is for the network, then we need to be able to compute the range of IP addresses that we will be able to find with this as well.

Bit Borrowing

Let us suppose that we are working with a process where we need to come up with 30 subnets that are in our 130.1.0.0 network. We would first have to go through and compute the bits that should be borrowed in order to come up with the right subnet mask. To know the number of bits here, we need to get the sum of lower-order bits, and then we can subtract one since we are not able to use the subnet of 0.

The ordered bits that we are able to work with are 128, 64, 32, 16, 8, 4, 2, and 1. The lower ordered are going to be counted from 1, 2, 4, and then the higher-ordered bits are counted from 128, 64, 16, and so on. Therefore, 30 subnets are going to be obtained by getting the sum of 1 + 2 + 4 + 8 + 16 minute 1. This gets us 31 − 1 and that equals 30. Counting from one to 16 this way is going to provide us with 5 bites so the number of bits that are borrowed here is going to be 5.

This is where we are going to be able to calculate out the host addresses that are in each subnet. We first need to remember that right from the beginning of our subnetting endeavor; we decided to work with 30 subnets for our 130.1.0.0 network. We then went through and borrowed out 5 bits from the third octet. Considering that the network ID is something that we are not able to touch at all, we only were able to work with 16 bits for the host addresses (sum of bits from the third and fourth octets, each with 8 bits), at the outset.

From there, we went through and borrowed another five bits from the third octet, which leaves us with only 3 bits to work with. This means that we are only going to be left with three bits from the third octet and then eight of these bits from the fourth octet. Adding in the fourth and the third octet, which is three plus 8, we are going to end up with 11 bits for the host address to work with here.

To help us to calculate out the number of host addresses that we are able to work with, we are going to 2 to the x power -2. X is going to be the number of available host addresses that we are able to use, which is going to be 11 here. When we finish this out, we are going to end up with the number of 2046, which is going to be how many hosts we are able to find for each of the subnets that we work with.

Determining the Host Ranges

To help us get going with this one, we are going to need to go through and look at the process for determining the mask of the subnet. We were able to use some of the higher ordered bits in order to determine what the value of our third octet in this mask is going to be.

First, though, are you able to remember the lowest of the higher ordered bits that we had? It was 8 if you need a refresher here. Therefore, we are going to use this as the lowest of the higher ordered bits as the increments that we can rely on with the third octet of the network address in order to obtain the first subnet ID. We will then continue with this all the way to the last of the 30 subnets. Keep in mind with this one that you are not able to have zero for the last portion of the address, and you are not allowed to have 255 at the end of any address either so do not let that happen.

Subnet Masks Changing

The next thing that we need to handle is the subnet mask changing. The subnet mask on each of the gadgets that we are working with needs to come in as equivalent to each other, or you are going to end up with a lot of issues in what they are able to take in and what it is not able to take in. The significant part that we need to consider here is that all of the machines in the subnet need to come with a cover that is similar.

All of the doors and the switches need to come with their ports arranged in the right way. This is done to make sure that they are able to coordinate the subnet so that they are going to be connected to by means of that port. You are also able to have various masks that show up in the variety of subnets that we work with. However, we also need to have a switch or a door with two addressable ports. One needs to happen on each of the subnets here.

Despite the fact that these covers for the subnet are going to usually be set out to be separated at each byte point, it is also possible to set them up to isolate inside of a byte. This is more enthusiastically to work out as it must be done depending on the twofold figures that are inside of the byte. This one is going to be up to you whether you would like to take on that extra work to get it done.

Another option to work with is utilizing any of the IP addresses that can extend that you need inside to give you the door to what you are doing. Otherwise, you may need to take the time to apply for and see if you are able to get an open IP address class permit that is going to suit the system that you are in. better to set up a passage or a switch with the Network Address Translation, or NAT, and simply utilize the IP address that is allotted by the Internet service provider, or ISP, you are working with.

Now, we will also find that there are going to be three explicit location gatherings that have been saved exclusively for this kind of inner use. It is suggested that you work with these as switches to the internet and so they are set up to NOT advance on location inside of these extents. This means that any traffic that is accidentally let out is going to be dumped before it is able to go anywhere.

VLAN

Another topic that we need to spend some time on here is going to be the VLAN, which is known as the Virtual Local Area Network. This is going to be a kind of network that has been switched and is going to be segmented logically using a project team, an application, or a function. The logical segmentation is going to be done without consideration of the physical location of those who are going to use them.

To keep it simple, these VLANs are going to be similar to what we would imagine with a physical LAN. The main difference is that the VLANs are going to allow some end stations to be grouped regardless of whether or not they are on the same physical segment or not. The VLAN is able to accommodate any form of switch module pot that we want to use. In addition, multicast, broadcast, and unicast data packets are relayed and swamped to end stations only in a given VLAN to keep them safe.

Each of these is going to be taken as a more logical network. Packets that are fated for stations that are not in the VLAN have to be forwarded through the router to help them reach their destination. One thing to note here is that the VLAN is something that can be associated back with the subnets that we were talking about with our IP addresses.

Chapter 6: Common Networking Protocols

The next thing that we need to look at is some of the common networking protocols that are going to be found on many networks out there. All of the different things that you want to accomplish when it comes to your network will need to follow some kinds of regulations and rules in order to be successful, and it is important that you go through the right procedure in a strict and secure manner to make sure your network not only works well but that it is also going to stay safe from attacks along the way.

The success that we have seen with networking and its concept is going to be due in big part to the constant initiatives of refinement that we are able to see in the environment of networking through networking models and some of the protocols that are there as well.

This brings us to the idea of network protocols and why these are so important. The network protocols are going to refer back to some of the rules and regulations that are present on many networks. The reason that they are so important is that they are going to ensure that the network is able to perform in the manner that it should and that you see the efficiency that you would like in the system as a whole.

Network services are basically going to be attainable due to the existence of these protocols. In addition, having some level of consistency in the standards of these networks are going to be sustainable due to the network protocols.

Given some of the different models, which are just two network models, it is no doubt that along the way, we are going to find some dissimilarities in how we are able to implement the concept of networking. This is why the OSI networks and the TCP/IP options are going to show many variations in how they perform. This is most notable to the network protocols that each one is going to spend some time on.

The TCP/IP Model

For now, we are going to take a quick look at how we are able to work with the TCP/IP model. This is one of the original models, and it is going to stand out a bit from the OSI model that some networkers have worked with in the past. To start with, there are going to be four main layers that we are able to see when it comes to this model, and they include:

1. The network access
2. The internet
3. The application layer
4. The transport layer

There are going to be some different network protocols that we will see with each of the layers, and it is the responsibility of each protocol to come in and play the right role in the process, ensuring that each layer is going to function in the manner that we want. The sum total of these layers and their functions will complete the concept of the network and the primary role of connecting the devices, sharing all of the resources, and facilitating some of the communication of the network as well.

Protocols of the Application Network

First on the list is going to be some of the protocols that we are able to work with when it comes to the application layer. This is going to be the top layer that we are able to see with this model. It is also going to be known as the process layer. It will be the one that can help to handle the issues of representation and some of the higher-level protocols as well. This layer will permit some interaction between the user and the applications that are present there.

When the application layer protocol is in need of communicating back with another layer in the application, it will work with the transport layer to make this happen. Keep in mind with this one that even though we can look to the name, not all applications out there can be installed on this layer. It is only going to be the applications that are able to interact with our communication system that we are able to place on this layer.

For example, it is impossible for us to install a text editor to this layer, but we can work with a web browser that relies on HTTP on this layer if we would like. The reason for this is that the browser is able to interact directly with the network that we focus on. The HTTP has to be noted as an application layer protocol if we want it to work well.

Transport Layer Protocols

In addition to working with the application network of our process, it is time to look at the transport layer. This one will make sure that the communication that has to happen with the application layer will actually go through. If you are familiar with the OSI model, this transport layer is going to match up with the transport layer that we are able to see in the OSI model.

In this layer, we are going to make sure that the end to end communication that needs to happen between the hosts is actually able to happen. It is also going to be the part that is responsible for making sure that error-free data delivery will happen. In addition, in the end, this layer will make sure that the application layer is protected from any data complexities.

Protocols of the Internet Layer

Next on the list will be some of the protocols that we are going to see with the internet layer. At some point, your network is going to spend some time online. Whether this is through email or doing a search or even shopping, you need to have some protocols in place to deal with it.

The internet layer is going to have its functions run parallel to the functions of the network layer that we find in the OSI method.

The protocol definition is going to start showing up when we work with the internet layer as well. Keep in mind that these are the protocols that are responsible for the logical data transmission that happens over the whole network.

Several different protocols are going to be available when we are looking through the internet layer. However, we just need to focus on one, known as the IP Protocol. This is going to be the protocol that is the most responsible for helping to deliver packets of data to the destination host from another host. The layer is going to be able to accomplish this when it checks for some of the addresses of IP that are found in the headers of the packet.

There are going to be two versions of this kind of protocol that includes IPv4 and IPv6. Most websites are going to rely on the former, but there has been a rising interest in the IPv6 option as well. This is because the addresses that are available to IPv4 are more limited in number, and IPv6 will not limit the number so we have more options along the way.

Link Layer Protocols

The next thing that we are going to look at here is the network access layer or the link layer. This one is going to be a kind of combination between the data link layer and the physical layer. This layer is able to check out the addressing of the hardware that we want to work with. The protocols that are present in this access layer will make sure that the data we are trying to send off can be physically transmitted as well.

The Protocol for Frame Relay

The last part that we are going to look at here is the Frame Relay Protocol. This is going to be a kind of packet-switched communication service. It is going to run from the LAN to the WAN and some of the backbone kind of networks that you have. We will find that this is split up into two layers that we can work with, including the data link layer and the physical layer.

The frame relay option is going to be able to implement all of the protocols that are standard when we are in the physical layer, and then these can be applied to the data link layer later on when we are ready. The virtual circuits can join one router over to more than one remote network if we want. In addition, in many cases, the permanent virtual circuits will make the connectivity a reality. The switched virtual circuits can also be used with this one.

To make this work, we will have to rely on fast packet technology and X.25. Data transmission in this option is going to be done through the encapsulation of packets into many sized frames. A lack of error-detection is going to be the cause of the high rate of transmission that we are going to see with this. Then, the endpoints are able to come in and perform functions to correct the errors, along with some of the retransmissions of the frames that have been dropped.

The two main frame relay devices that we are able to use in some of the work that we are doing here will include data terminating equipment and data circuiting terminating equipment.

As we can see, many parts will come together when we talk about some of the protocols that are necessary for our network to behave and work well. These rules and regulations are going to seem like they are stringent and hard to work with, and like they may take some of the fun out of the process. However, in reality, they are there to keep the network safe and ensure that it is going to complete the work that it should along the way.

Chapter 7: Internet Essentials We Need to Know

You will not be able to spend a lot of time on your network without accessing the internet at some point. There are many networks that spend a lot of time online and working with the internet, and being able to handle this and understanding how the internet works, and how your network is able to interact back with the network will be essential to ensuring that it is all works smoothly. That is why we are going to spend some time in this chapter looking at the basics of the internet and how it fits into some of the networking that we talk about here.

Internet Basics

In this section, we are going to take a look at some of the basic concepts of technology that are important to understanding how the Internet works, and we will also discuss some of the options so that we can connect to the information superhighway, ensuring that all of the people who are on your network are able to share information, conduct research online, surf the web, and communication with email. However, we need to start out with a bit more about the technical terms of the Internet first.

Just like it is not necessary for us to go through and know some of the inner works of a combustion engine just to get into a car and drive it, it is also not going to be imperative that we understand all of the aspects of how the Internet will work before we are able to really take advantage of all the neat things that it is able to offer.

With that said, though, it never hurts for us to discuss this and examine some of the concepts and the terms that relate back to the Internet. The first one on the list is the TCP/IP. This stands for Transmission Control Protocol/Internet Protocol. This is going to be the main group of rules, which are known as protocols in our networks, that are going to define how a device, whether they are the same or very different, are able to connect and then communicate with one another.

This protocol is going to work the best because it is able to determine the best transmission path that is available so that the data can safely and effectively travel. Rather than sending out all of the data in just one big chunk, the protocol is able to break up that data into some smaller packets ahead of time. These packets are then going to travel through a variety of paths in the hopes of finding the right destination. In addition, when they arrive, they are going to be reassembled in the right order for success.

To make sure that the packets are going to find their way to the right destination that we want, the packets are going to contain both the source address and the destination address. This is going to be some information that is stored in the header or the envelope of each packet. The TCP port of this kind of protocol is going to be the one that is able to control the breakdown of the data when it comes to the sending in, and then the reassembly when it gets to the right location. Then the IP is going to be the part that is able to handle the routing of these data packets.

Then we are able to move on to the DNS. This is going to be for the domain name system. When you enter in the domain name of any site that you want to go and visit, the browser you are on is going to initiate a session that has the DNS server either locally or online in order to find the right IP address that is associated back with that domain name again.

The servers of the DNS are going to work with a hierarchical lookup for the IP addresses with the help of the domain name associated and the help of the IP address of the site that you would like to visit. If the DNS server on the computer is linked to can't determine what the IP address of the domain name you chose is, then the DNS server is going to try and look on higher servers until it finds the right one or it ends up erroring out in the process.

Once the IP address has been found, then the computer can go through, communicate, and locate the computer that has the right website that you need. The first DNS server is going to then store this association in the memory for a time in case you, and sometimes someone else, it serves ends up visiting that site later. This is only going to store the associations that you use on a frequent basis because it can look up the ones that it does not know on the higher-level DNS servers.

We can also work with the subnet masks. This is going to be the number that is going to be applied within a host configuration file that is going to allow us to divide the IP class C network until it is into some networks that can be routed separately. When we look at some of the home networks on a larger network of ISP's, the subnet mask is going to be something like 255.255.255.9, because the home networks are not going to be the ones that are split into some separate segments with internal routers.

When we focus on an office building and some of the business environment, subnets are going to be used to detach traffic into networks that are physically isolated in order to retain some of the traffic for data on the low and to enhance some of the performance for access to the local servers and the peripherals. The data traffic that is destined to go to another WAN or subnet will need to first do this through the router.

We also can take a look at the World Wide Web and what this is all about. Just like with a living creature, what we know as the Web is going to shift all of the time. Networks are changed and added. In addition, the evolution of the Internet both in the geographic scope and in the audience who uses it will offer every linked object with the potential to communicate in a manner that was impossible in the past. If you find that your use of this is limited to just getting emails and downloading the necessary information, you are barely taking advantage of all that the web is able to offer to us.

There are a lot of ways that we are able to utilize the web, including to inform, exchange ideas, goods, and services, and even education. There really are no limits when it comes to this World Wide Web and learning how to use it properly is going to be important to help us see some results in the process.

Now, you need to make sure that you connect your network over to the web in order to get this to work. Connecting your network or even a subnetwork of yours to the Internet is going to stretch the reach of your home or office network to any place you would like around the world. For less than $120 a month for most of the markets in the United States, you are able to obtain your own connection to the internet that is going to run at decent speeds and will include five static IP addresses that you can use.

These addresses are useful because they have the power to enhance your ability to get the most out of your Internet connection. This is because, in order to work with a lot of your resources, like webcams and web servers, you need to make sure that there is, at a minimum, one IP address that is static and will be visible online as well.

In addition, this kind of IP address can be what you work with to enable the VPN clients to connect to your network resources. Without this kind of address, much of the communication that you want to do with the outside world is going to have some limits. With the static IP address, though, you will find that your network can grow, becoming a blog, a TV station, a radio station, a client-services provider, a web site or anything else that you want.

The web is going to be your network's window to the world. Not only are you able to use it to see out into the world, obtaining quite a bit of data from the web, but others will also be able to use this to see in so that you are able to share information of your choosing with an audience worldwide. Adding in some of your own resources to this kind of communication is going to make sure that your company is able to provide value while increasing how useful the web is for others who use it.

We can often guess some of the main uses of the internet since we have been consumers of it for quite some time at this point. You will find that there are many uses that come with working online, and being able to set it up in the right manner to provide the best benefits to your customers, or just for your own network, is important.

For example, we can work with the internet to find entertainment, to publish information and content, to talk with others online in email or social media, to do surveillance, to learn something new, and so much more. There really are no limitations when it comes to what the internet is able to do for your needs, and making sure that you use it for your network, especially your business network, in the proper manner, is going to be so important along the way as well.

How to Pick Out an Internet Plan

The internet plan that you pick out for your network, whether it is an office or a personal network, is going to be important. Two main parts need to come into play when you want to be able to establish the necessary home access to the Internet. You need to have at least one computer that is able to get onto the Internet, and you also need to be able to purchase a plan from an ISP or an Internet Service Provider.

The plans that are available for you to pick from are really going to vary based on where you live. For example, rural areas and even some suburban areas are going to have fewer options than you can find in cities. It also depends on the kind of media for communication that you would like to use and what options the ISP decides to give to you. However, some of the features that you should look for in any plan that you want to work with includes:

1. Email addresses
2. Customer service support
3. Internet speed
4. How much it costs
5. The equipment that your ISP is going to provide to you
6. The nature of the address that they are going to provide to you and whether this is going to be a dynamic or a static IP address.
7. Whether there is the option for a complimentary Wi-Fi address if this is important to your business.
8. If you are able to work with webpage hosting
9. If there is anything to help with the transmission media that you want to use.

Once you have the internet plan set up, it is time to learn how to get the connectivity that you need to the internet. To connect your computer to the internet, you need to be able to choose from the plans for services that are found in your particular area. Once you have evaluated the plans and the media options, then you can go through some of the following points to get the Internet set up.

First, we can consider using dial-up. Of course, this one is obsolete any more, and there are likely few ISP's that will provide this. However, if you are in a rural area, this may be the only option that is available for you to use. When you connect your computer using this method, you are doing so over the plain old telephone service line. There are a few common scenarios that you are able to work with on this one including:

1. You can hook up your laptop or your computer working on the modem that is built-in.
2. You can work with an external dial-up modem that is going to be connected back to the USB port.
3. Use can work with some of the modems that are able to connect us back to the serial port that is 9-pins.

Another option to work with is to handle cables. This is going to be a popular choice to connect to the internet. It is likely that your home or your small office is going to come with a connection for television service, so making the addition of the cable modem you need for the internet simple. This service is going to be much faster than other options, and these bundles can also come with internet phone service and a good cable package, too if that is important to you.

The next option that we are able to focus on is Wi-Fi. Connecting in a wireless fashion to the internet is going to be simple, but before you are able to do that, you need to make sure that your network has a router or a gateway that is designed to handle some of these wireless connections. In addition, any of the computers on the network are going to need to have some Wi-Fi capabilities that are in it, or if you are working with a notebook computer or a laptop, there needs to be a spot for a wireless Wi-Fi card to make this work.

If your workstations or the computers that you want to use are not configured to work with Wi-Fi, this does not mean that all hope is lost here. There are going to be many companies out there who can provide us with devices that support these wireless connections. These are going to be portable wireless NICs that we can plus into our USB port or our Ethernet port.

In addition, the final option that we have when it comes to connecting our network over to the internet is to rely on DSL. Using DSL to help you connect to the Internet with the help of some standard phone lines is going to provide us with the advantage of being able to access the internet with higher speeds compared to the option of dial-up, but it does assume that we currently live in an area where this kind of service is going to be available for us to use (it is not available in many rural areas).

In addition, we will find that the dial-up connection that we talked about before is going to rely on the analog or the audio band on a phone line, data that is found on the DSL Internet connection is going to pass over the wire pair, usually at a frequency that is higher than others. This means that users are able to work with the phone line while still being able to work with and use the Internet in the manner that they would like. This is something useful for many companies and is one of the main ways that people are able to access the internet in our modern world.

As we can see, there are a lot of benefits to working with the internet, and whether you are creating the network for your own personal use or you need to use it for your business, having a good understanding of how the internet works and what we are able to do with it is going to be important to use seeing some of the success that we want. There are many reasons why we would want to be able to go online, search the internet, share information, and conduct business through communicating in various means. There is no tool out there that can help your business to grow and see success as much as the internet can, regardless of your business type or the industry you are in.

Chapter 8: Virtualization and How It Fits In

If you have spent any amount of time working in your business, then it is likely that you have heard a bit about the idea of virtualization architecture, and cloud computing as well. Both of these are important ideas for us to consider and learning how to add them to any network that we want to create, and seeing how they can make our lives easier is so important. And that is why we are going to spend some time in this chapter taking a look at two important topics to our network; the idea of virtualization architecture and the idea of cloud computing and how these will be able to help our network succeed.

What Does Cloud Computing Mean?

Cloud computing is going to refer to the process of delivering IT resources through the internet based on the demand for those items. It is often going to be implemented with the idea of pay as you go pricing. The concept of cloud computing is used by many businesses, and it is really going to seek to offer us a solution to IT infrastructure at larger levels while keeping some of the costs lower in the process.

For small, and even for some big, IT companies that are still relying on older and more traditional methods to operate, they will often need to work with a server to help carry out the variety of tasks that need to be done. Setting up this server room is going to require that we have a lot of skilled personnel, lots of servers, switches, modems, and other resources to finish the network. That is just some of the IT requirements, not to mention the other parts that need to come to play as well.

Traditional methods are going to require a lot of human input, some expensive equipment, and other necessities to get it up and running. Moreover, these are all going to require a lot of money in the process as well. To get the server set up and to ensure that it is fully functional, the company or individual has to be willing to pretty much break the bank. This is worth it, but not all companies, especially the smaller ones, are going to be able to afford to make this happen at all.

However, this is no longer the norm since we now have the idea of cloud computing to work with. Cloud computing is going to help individuals figure out ways to cut down on the costs of infrastructure by eliminating the need for that company to go out and purchase equipment that is expensive and spending a lot of money on personnel that is needed for the management and administration of our IT resources.

Characteristics of Cloud Computing

There are a lot of characteristics that we are able to explore when it comes to working with the idea of cloud computing. Some of the most common ones are going to include:

1. Cloud computing is going to operate in a computing environment that is distributed. This is going to make resources sharing easier to work with overall.

2. Cloud computing is going to help minimize some of the chances that there will be an infrastructural failure, thanks to the existence of many servers. This ensures that the infrastructure that we are working with is going to be more reliable for some of our IT operations.

3. Cloud computing is going to allow us to have some large-scale and on-demand provisions of the resources of IT without the need for engineers and other professionals that would be necessary for other situations.

4. Cloud computing is going to enable a lot of users to share their resources, and they will be able to work in a more efficient manner by sharing the same infrastructure in the process.

5. This kind of computing is going to work to eliminate some of the distance or physical location concerns because users are able to access the resources and the systems that are stored here no matter where they are located.

6. Maintaining the applications of cloud computing will be easier since they do not need to be installed on each computer on the network.

7. This kind of computing is going to reduce the operating cost that we see with an organization because it allows the company to get the benefits that they want with this process, without needing to go through the process of setting up their own infrastructure. This is going to be too much of an undertaking, setting up that system for your own needs, for most companies. In addition, it allows that company to come in and only pay for the resources and the services that they need.

8. Cloud computing is going to rely on a pay per use kind of model for the different services. It is going to be a really convenient manner for us to use and can be really helpful when the user only needs to bring out the resource one time.

Instead of installing a whole suite and having to deal with a costly software for the computer of each employee on your network, it is possible to just come in with a single application where all of the users are going to login and access the exact resources that they need to work with. The application is going to come in and allow the users access to the web-based service that is going to hold all of the applications that we need for the execution of our tasks. Remote servers are also going to do everything while we manage and administer them through a third party. This is going to be known as cloud computing.

When we look at cloud computing, the local computers are not going to be that worried about how the heavy lifting works. The remote servers are able to do this by running all of the software needed and holding onto some of the bulky files. These will minimize the demands on the software and hardware of the user along the way. Even a not so expensive network is able to run the software that we need for cloud computing, and it is going to eliminate any needs that we have to purchase most of the software applications since we are able to access them through the cloud.

What is Virtualization?

Now that we have had some time to look closer at cloud computing, it is time for us to look at how we are able to work with the idea of virtualization. This is going to be a process by which a virtual version of something is going to be created. When we look at computing, this could involve the virtualization of an operating system, a server, storage device, network resources, and even the desktop that we are working with.

Technically, we are able to take this process of virtualization and refer to it as a technique that is going to permit the sharing of one instance of a physical resource or even an application among multiple users or groups. This is going to be a technique that will involve the assignment of a logical name over to the physical storage of a given resource or application, and then it will offer a pointer to the application or the resources as it is required.

This brings us to the idea of what types of virtualization that we can work with. There are several categories that we are able to work with when it comes to virtualization, but the first one we are going to focus on is server virtualization. When a VMM or virtual machine manager is directly installed to our server, then we are working with the process known as server virtualization. This is going to be an important option to work with because it allows us a method to subdivide a physical server into more than one server, based on demand, and it works to help with load balancing.

Then we can move on to the idea of storage virtualization. This one is a bit different in that it is the process that will help us to group the multiple storage devices that we have from before into a network so that they will appear like they are just one single device for storage. There are a lot of software applications that can be used to help us implement this kind of visualization. This is going to be an important type to work with because it is important for the backup or the recovery of your network.

We can also work with the Operating System Virtualization. This is when the VMM is going to be installed directly to your operating system for the machine that you are using as the host. Unlike some of the hardware virtualization, the VMM will not be installed over to the hardware. This is a good type of virtualization that can come in useful when there is a big need to test out our applications on the different operating systems that are available.

Next on the list is the hardware virtualization. This is where the virtual machine software that we want to use is installed right onto the system hardware. A hypervisor is going to be the part that is responsible for monitoring and controlling the processor, memory, and hardware resources that you see. We are able to go through and install some different operating systems on this and will use it to run quite a few of the other applications that you want, once the process is done. Hardware virtualization is going to be important for a lot of the server platforms since the control over a virtual machine is not going to be as difficult as the control over a physical server.

How Visualization Works in Cloud Computing

The next thing that we need to look at here is how we are able to work with virtualization when we handle cloud computing. Virtualization is going to be a potent concept when it comes to the cloud computing that we talked about before. Normally when we work with cloud computing, users are going to have to share the resources that are available in the clouds. For example, applications and files are going to be a few of the resources that are sharable and that we are able to store in our cloud.

With the help of virtualization here, the user will be provided with a platform that will allow them to share these resources in a more practical manner. The primary goal that we are going to see with virtualization is that it is going to offer applications with their standard versions over to the users who are on that cloud. Then, when a new version of the application has been released, the users are able to look to the developer of the software to get that new release.

This is going to be possible, but often it is going to turn into a more hectic affair if all of the users have to download the new version from the central server. To help us deal with this kind of issue, the software and the servers of virtualization can be maintained through a third party, with a fee, but the cloud users are able to efficiently and quickly access the new releases of the software.

What this all means is that with virtualization, we are able to run several operating systems on just one machine that is already able to share the resources needed for the hardware here. This is a helpful technique to work with because it allows us to pool together some of the resources of the network and will make it easier to share them to different users in a convenient manner, and for less money overall.

While we are here, we need to look at some of the components that are found with our server computer. These are going to include things like the power supply, memory, video cards, network connection, processor, motherboard, and storage drives.

There are also a few parts of software that will fit in with virtualization that we need to know about. Sometimes it is going to depend on the program that you would like to work within particular, but there are a lot of great options. For example, we can work with Apple-Boot camp, Veertu-for MAC, Redhat Virtualization, Microsoft Hyper-V, QEMU, Oracle Virtualization, Parallels Desktop, VMWare Workstation, and VMWare Fusion.

The Types of Cloud Services to Use

There are a few options that we are able to work with when it is time to handle the cloud and bring this into your network and the way that you run your business. Cloud computing is nice in many ways, but one of the benefits it that it is going to provide us with some on-demand cloud services that we can access through the internet. There are options to choose from for these cloud services, but some of the most popular options are going to include:

1. Amazon Web Services
2. Google Cloud
3. Microsoft Azure

Should I Choose Private or Public Clouds?

The next question that you may have when it comes to working with your network is whether you should work with a public cloud or if a private cloud is the best option to go with. The public cloud is going to offer some solutions to hosting that is different compared to the hosting with a private cloud, and often the biggest difference is how both of these solutions are going to be managed. Let us look at each one of these and see how we are able to work with them.

First on the list is the public cloud services. This hosting solution is going to mean that our data is stored and then managed by the provider of that cloud. These providers are going to be the ones that are completely responsible for maintaining the data centers that the data you send over is going to be held. Many times a company is going to favor this kind of cloud hosting because the costs for managing it are easier to handle.

However, there are some situations where the security and the safety of your data in this kind of cloud could be at a higher risk. The provider of the cloud has the responsibility to keep this information safe and secure, even though it is a public cloud, but things can happen. If the security of your data is important, then it may be a good idea to work with another cloud option to ensure that no one is able to get onto the data you are using.

Then there are the private cloud services. With these, the hosting is going to leave the responsibility for the management, and the maintenance of the cloud service will be inside the companies own authority and arrangement. This is sometimes known as an internal cloud or an enterprise cloud. The company or the enterprise in question is going to need to host its own service for the cloud behind a firewall that they have in place to make sure that it is safe.

Though the security and the safety of the data can be provided at a much higher level than it has been done with some of the public cloud hosting solutions, the requirements that come with this one are often too costly for most businesses to try and take on. It is also going to require that we employ the right kind of personnel, those with a lot of education and experience in the world of IT, in order to handle the cloud. This means that while you may end up with more security, the operational costs often jump up quite a bit in the process.

For a lot of the networks out there, working with a good cloud or virtualization software is going to be one of the best options that we are able to work with. You will find that this will allow us to store some of our important files and documents inside of the cloud, and be able to reach it no matter where we are located.

Many companies like to work with this option because it allows them to hold onto the data that they need, and can make it easier to share the documents and important information to people all over the world, without them having to hold onto it all, or worry about the hardware, software, and personnel requirements that are there for making this work on their own. Even if your business is not large, you will find that working with virtualization on the crowd could be the best option to help you see success.

Chapter 9: Implementing the Windows System

There are many different types of systems that we are able to work with when it comes to handling our networking. Moreover, all of them are going to come with certain benefits, and maybe a few negatives that we need to be aware of. However, for our needs, we are going to look at how we are able to benefit from one operating system, in particular, known as the Windows System.

General Features of Windows

Throughout the years, Microsoft has been able to release a series of different operating systems, thanks to the advancement in technology. In addition, in each new version that has come out, we have seen some great new features and some corrections to errors that the previous version may have had to deal with. There are a lot of different versions of the Windows systems that we are able to work with, and some of the most well-known out of all of these include:

1. DOS, or Disk Operating System
2. Windows 95 and 98
3. Windows ME Millennium edition
4. Windows NT, or New Technology
5. Windows 2000

6. Windows XP
7. Windows Vista
8. Windows 7
9. Windows 8
10. Windows 10

As of the writing of this guidebook, Windows 10 was the current and the latest version out of the operating series that Microsoft spent their time on. This one was released back in November of 2018, and it is going to have a lot of general features that you would expect with a good operating system, plus a lot of other great things that we are able to enjoy when we choose this kind of operating system over some of the others.

What to Expect in Windows?

With this in mind, we need to take some time to look at a few of the general features that are present with this kind of system. Many operating systems are going to have the features that come pretty standard with using them, and Windows is no different along the way. Some of the general features that we are able to enjoy with a Windows system and from having this on our network will include:

1. The input and the output are going to be controlled by the operating system.

As the access that you get to a device is going to be essential so that we can work with operations of input and output, we have to remember that it is going to be the coordinates of the operating system that will help to run the whole device. In addition, this is going to allow the users to read information from print information or other websites from the comfort of their own home if they would like.

This is just the start of what we are able to do with all of this, though. When you decide to work with this kind of feature, you are also going to be able to read the information and then redistribute it on the system that your computer runs through and send it off to others. In addition, all of this is possible thanks to the fact that the Windows operating system is going to be the part that helps to control the input and the output of our computers.

2. It can multi-task

Another thing that we will be able to see when it comes to working with the Windows operating system is that you are able to take some of the actions that require multitasking and get them to perform in a smooth manner, while also getting it done at the same time. When you want to have two programs running at the same time, or you would like to complete the specific actions at the same time, then this is going to be the tool that you will appreciate the most from the Windows system.

For example, if you are working with a network that has the Windows 10 operating system, you will find that it is able to handle more than one task at a time. It will be able to read off all of the information that is found on the disk, display some of the printing results that you need, and can run some user programs that are more complex, all at the same time. In addition, this system can be used as an example of multi-programming and multi-tasking all at the same time.

3. It can help us to manage our work

Without even realizing it at the time, you will often work with an operating system to help plan out some of the tasks that should happen on your computer system, as well as some of the tasks that need to happen with the hardware devices. This is true whether we are working with the output or the input for either of these.

This is actually one of the main features that you are going to see when you work on the Windows operating system, and it is going to allow you to really get things done, will ensure that the system is going to behave in the manner that you would like, and so much more along the way.

For example, this feature from Windows is going to help create the order that you need to handle any processing program. It can also work on defining the sequence in which a computer will take ahold of the tasks that need to be done, and pick out when that task should be done

4. It can help to allocate all of the resources of the computer

Another benefit that we are going to enjoy when it comes to working with the Windows system is that it is able to allocate out all of the resources that we need to use along the way. The Windows operating system is a good one to work with because it can help to monitor the execution of all programs that are found on the system. This is going to be considered one of the general features that we are able to see with this kind of system, and it is going to make sure that everything is done in an efficient manner on your system.

Taking the time to allocate all of the resources on our computer systems on our own is never a good idea. It takes too long to handle all of this, and we often do not understand the most efficient or effective manner in which to do this on our own. Having the operating system do this for us, without us having to think through it or worry about it at all, is going to be imperative to us seeing some of the results that we want along the way.

However, to take on these tasks, the operating system is going to create a table that is able to combine all of the programs from that device in one place. Using this kind of feature, you will find that the computer is not able to use the hardware device if that is not one of the options that are available. This table is going to help the system to know whether the device is available to work with or not.

In a similar manner, the operating system, thanks to this feature, is going to monitor all types of applications and devices working in a particular system and will allocate some resources back to them along the way as well. This can help to save us a lot of time and will ensure that we are getting the system to work well, without having to do the work on our own.

5. It is able to launch the programs we need.

This operating system is going to be able to function as the necessary launcher so that you have a way to open up any program that you would like to work with, organize all of the documents you need, and transfer data when it is needed. The GUI's that are found with our system will make it easier for us to click on the image that comes with a program or a document, and we are able to click on these to get them to open up and work the way that we want.

All programs are going to be tied up to the operating system in order to function. This means that each of the systems that you want to work with is going to come with its own software, which is why you are not able to really run a Windows program on a computer that has a Mac system, and we can't go through and do it the opposite way either.

6. It is going to come with a core that we can focus our work on.

The Core is going to be considered one of the key features that we are able to work with on the Windows operating system. These cores will provide a good way for the different applications in a system to interact with one another. This core is also going to manage the RAM that is able to store some of the information that the software needs to function.

Today, the monolithic nuclei are going to be one of the most popular cores that are used in different operating systems that we are able to find around the world. In addition, most of the operating systems and the cores they work with are device drivers that are going to control the hard disks, will control monitors, and all of the other hardware devices that we want to focus on.

7. It can provide us with the connection that we need between the software and the hardware.

Our networks will be some combination of hardware and software in order to make the computer function. One is not going to be more important than the others are, and we need a good combination of both to make them work. In addition, the operating system that we use will be able to provide us with the connection that we need between the hardware and the software.

One of the other general features that we will notice when working with the Windows system is that it is going to make sure that we are going to see a steady connection between the user interface, software, and hardware. In addition, if you try to work without it, you are not going to be able to use the resources of the computer at all in order to perform the tasks that you want.

As we can see, we can see many benefits when working with the Windows system. This is one of the best options that we can choose when it comes to handling our networks and will ensure that we are able to get the software and the hardware to work in the manner that we would like to work with.

The Benefits of Using Windows

Now it is time for us to look at some of the benefits that are present when it comes to working with the Windows system in the first place. There are many options that we can choose from when it is time to pick out the operating system we want to work with, so why would the Windows system be one of the best ones for us to look at along the way. Some of the main benefits that we can enjoy when working on the Windows operating system will include:

1. It is an easy system to work with: When compared to some of the other operating systems, Windows is easy to work with. It was built on the idea of GUI, or graphical user interface, which makes life easier. Rather than having to type out the codes that we want to use on Windows, we can click on an icon and get to the file or the application that we want to use.

2. It is easy to get the software: One of the reasons that Windows is so popular is that the availability and ease of gathering up the software were easy as well. You are able to use this operating system for personal and business use, and there are plenty of options when it comes to finding the right software for your needs.

3. It is the choice of other manufacturers: While you can certainly take the time to go through and make changes to the system you are on, many of the computers that you are able to purchase on the market today will come with Windows systems on them. This is because it is easy to

work with and less expensive than other options, so it is the option you are most likely to encounter as well.

4. The games are awesome to use. While this is not the top reason for businesses working with the Windows system, gaming is important for many people who are choosing the system they want. If you are interested in working on gaming and all that this entails, you will find that the Windows system is going to be able to provide us with lots of games to choose from, and a good interface that makes the process of gaming easier than ever as well.

These are just a few of the benefits that we are able to see when it is time to work with the Windows system. In addition, if you have worked with this system in the past for any reason, it is likely that you know a few other benefits that you can put here as well. Using this kind of system is simple to work with, is found on a lot of the different computers and hardware devices that you are looking for, and so much more. That is why many networks are going to spend their time learning about this system and how they can use it for their needs as well.

Implementing Windows Distributed Network

Traditionally, there was going to be a monolithic kind of system that would run through more than one computer, and having this there meant that we needed to take the time to separate out the components for the client from the components for the server. In these systems, the client component is going to be the one that will handle all of the interfaces for the user, and the server would be able to handle all of the processing on the back-end, such as printing and database access.

As computers proliferated and more people started to use them, they dropped in cost, and became connected by some ever-higher bandwidth networks, splitting up the software systems into more than one component was something that was more convenient than ever before. With this system, each component was going to start running on a different computer, and it is going to be responsible for having its own specialized function to perform with.

This approach is more simplified when it comes to administration, management, development, and it can provide us with more robustness and performance on our system than before, which is going to be great news. This works so well because the failure that can happen on one computer is not going to be enough to disable the entire system. The rest of it is going to work well, without ruining the whole system on this kind of network.

In many situations of networking, the system is going to appear to the client more as an opaque cloud that is going to work on performing the operations that are necessary, even though this distributed system is going to be composed of nodes that are on their own but can work with one another.

The opacity that we are going to see with this cloud is often maintained because the operations of computing are going to be invoked on behalf of the client. Because of this, the clients are able to find one of the modes, which is a computer, inside of that cloud, and then will request a given operation. In performing this operation, the computer is then able to work with the other computers and utilize their functionality inside of the cloud, without having to expose any of the additional steps or the computer on which they were carried out, over to the client at all.

With this, all in place, the mechanics that we are going to see with this kind of cloud-like and distributed system is going to be changed and broken down into a lot of different packet exchanges, or conversations that show up between the individual nodes that are there.

This kind of system is going to be used in many situations, but is possible that it is not going to come with clients and servers that are dedicated to each packet exchange. Even without this, though, it is important for us to remember that there is always going to be a caller, or an initiator, either of which is going to be known in this system as the client.

In addition to the client of the caller, we are going to have a recipient that gets the call, and we will call this the server in this kind of system. It is not necessary for us to always go with a packet exchange that is two-way when we talk about the request and reply format of this distributed system. This is because it is possible, and is often the case, that the messages we see are going to be sent out in one direction, and there will not be something sent back the other way at all.

One of the ways that we are able to implement some of the software that is in a distributed system is to work with some raw networking support. This approach is going to include things like GETs, POSTs, HTTP, named pipes, sockets, and so much more. All of these are going to be models that are able to force a developer to work with low-level programming primitives. In addition, this is going to be what, in one manner or another, which force the developer to really work with the NDR, or the network data representation, packaging data, failure conditions, managing the traffic on the network, the encryption and the protection of our data integrity, and so much more.

RPC is going to be what we need in order to work on a programming model where the programmer or the developer is going to be able to retain some of the granular control of the interactions in the network, especially the ones that happen between the server and the client through a rich API while saving some developers time because they don't need to work with the details and all of the burdens that this kind of distributed system is often going to introduce.

For example, think about the burden that is going to be associated back with all of the different approaches that can be used when it is time to protect the privacy and integrity when you exchange messages in one of these systems. We want to make sure that we are able to send out the messages that we need without running into issues with these messages getting into the wrong hands. This is something that any kind of network is going to rely on, and the Windows system is going to help us get this taken care of.

When considering the kind of network security that we need for the exchange of messages in this system, there are going to be different kinds of protections in place, whether these protections are stronger or weaker. There is no true network security, only some different packet-based security mechanisms that we are able to work with.

We will also see that there are security measures in other areas that we are able to rely on. We will find that there is security when it is time to identify the caller we are working with, which is going to be one that is weaker because we are able to change the contents of the packet while they are in transit. We can work with the security that is going to help us protect the integrity that we will see with the packet, without having to worry about protecting the privacy that comes with this, through a variety of hashes and signatures to get it all done. In addition, we can also work with the security that is going to make sure that the privacy of the message in that exchange thanks to the mechanisms that are used to help encrypt and hide the information.

Another burden that we are going to run into trouble when it comes to working with the implementation of a secure distributed system is that we need to find the right algorithms that are important to implement some of the security primitives that we need. These are going to include things like authentication, signing, and encryption, to name a few. The developer is able to implement all of the algorithms, but doing these is often difficult to work with, can bring in a lot of potential issues along the way, and can be risky since the resulting algorithms are often going to have some small, but important flaws insecurity that we are not able to recognize.

In addition, it is possible that the developer is going to use the available provider of security in order to implement the protection for the interactions for that network in this system. This can sometimes make it easier, but it can potentially bring in some more issues that we need to consider along the way.

With the help of RPC and the Windows system, we are going to find that both of the burdens that we talked about above are going to be resolved in an easy manner. A developer simply needs to be able to tell the RPC what security package it needs to rely on, and which protections of security need to be applied back to the message exchange when it comes to the identity tracking of the caller, the mutual authentication for both sides of the communication, the encryption, and the authentication.

RPC is going to be able to help us take care of these details, doing all of the work behind the scenes, without us knowing what is going on, and it is still going to provide the developer with the full control that they need. This allows us a way to fully pick out how the data is going to be protected based on our own needs as well.

There are many different things that we are able to work on when it comes to handling the Windows system, and making sure that it is going to work for our own network along the way. We can choose to go through and work with some of the other systems as well, and they will provide us with many benefits along the way too. However, the Windows system is the one that is used the most often for many networks, and it will be able to get all of the work done for you in no time.

Conclusion

Thank you for making it through to the end of *A Beginner's Guide to Mastering Computer Networking*, let's hope it was informative and able to provide you with all of the tools you need to achieve your goals whatever they may be.

The next step is to take some time and look through some of the different parts that show up on your own network as well. Many people do not take the time to learn much about their network. They utilize it and enjoy the network when it is working. However, they find that they do not know all that much about how to make the network work or how to handle the different protocols and more. For those who would like to be able to learn some more about these items so that they can better understand the network they are handling at the time, and who are ready to start taking control over their own network, this guidebook has the answers you need.

There are many different parts that we need to consider when it comes to implementing our network and ensuring that it behaves in the right manner. From looking through all of it to learn the different hardware components and even some of the safety protocols that ensure your network is going to behave in accordance to what we want to see online and elsewhere, this guidebook is going to walk us through the different parts of networking so we can learn how to make this work for us.

Whether you are working with a personal network or one that is supposed to help run a big business, you will find that networking is going to be similar in most of these systems. Yes, the larger systems will often come with more devices and a few more parts, but some of the pasts are going to be the same no matter what we use along the way. That is the beauty of what we learn about in this guidebook. It is going to help us to handle all networks, no matter the size, so we can get it to work properly.

There are many things that we are able to learn how to work with when it comes to networking, and this guidebook has taken some time to look through them so we can understand our network and make sure that it follows the rules and protocols that we want. When you are ready to learn more about networking for beginners, and to get your own system up and running, make sure to check out this guidebook to help.

Finally, if you found this book useful in any way, a review on Amazon is always appreciated!